into the dark

JESSICA HALE

ISBN: 978-1-7774918-2-6
Ebook: 978-1-7774918-4-0
Digital: 978-1-7774918-3-3

Editor: Emily S Hurricane
Graphic Design (Interior and Exterior): Jessica Hale
Exterior Photo: Vasyl Onyshchuk
Interior Photo: Lucas Pezeta

First Printing, 2022

into the dark

a guided shadow work journal

JESSICA HALE

Shadow Work is the path
of the heart warrior.
- Carl Jung

what is shadow work?

The phrase itself is referring to the practice of understanding the parts of ourselves that we hide. These are the sides or aspects of our personalities that we subconsciously reject and repress, which can result in a perceived perspective of who we actually are.

The term “Shadow Self” was named by Carl Jung, a 20th century psychologist. He describes the Shadow Self as the unconscious part of the personality that our conscious ego doesn’t want to identify in itself.

Shadow Work is where we bring the parts of us we keep hidden into the light.

This isn’t easy or something to take no notice of. We need to be kind to ourselves when we are healing, and Shadow Work at its core is healing the sides of our persona that we ignore and suppress. It can be scary to be open up to these sides of ourselves, but this is how we can become better and more aware versions of ourselves.

Self exploration of your Shadow Self is not to be considered a substitute for professional counseling or therapy. These prompts should be used to help aid in discovering who you are and in your own personal growth.

Your Shadow is all of the things,
'positive' and 'negative', that you've
denied about yourself and hidden
beneath the surface of the mask
you forgot that you're wearing.
- Oli Anderson

working on our shadow self

It's easy for someone to point out a fault in someone else, but far more difficult to do in ourselves.

Shadow Traits or Behaviors are an automatic and often unintentionally negative reaction to ideas, people, events or circumstances. These traits are often created in our childhoods when we are more susceptible and we're not fully able to understand the thought or opinion we're creating.

Shadow behaviors may include:

- Jealousy
- Anger or prone angry outbursts
- Stubbornness
- Egotism or self-centeredness
- Judgmental/Critical
- Feelings of competitiveness
- Overly defensive
- Manipulative/Gaslighting
- Narcissism
- Addiction

The shadow is needed now more than ever.
We heal the world when we heal ourselves,
and hope shines brightest when it
illuminates the dark.
- Sasha Graham

benefits of shadow work

Exploring your Shadow Self will give you a better understanding of who you are and what triggers you. This will allow you to better navigate your thoughts, emotions and reactions to situations and be able to more easily communicate while creating a foundation and clearer understanding of your own mental health.

By becoming more open-minded we are allowing ourselves to see our darker traits and acknowledge them and we can begin to accept them in others and won't feel triggered so easily as we become more grounded. This will enhance our relationships with others; romantic, friendly, mutual and professional relationships will benefit as we establish balance in all connections between us and others.

Ongoing Shadow Work is self-care and can become an ongoing tool for self-awareness and healing.

At times you have to find the untouched parts within yourself to be able to discover the true you on a deeper level.

- Etheria Divine

beginning your shadow work

No one is ever ready for a deep-dive of the soul. This journal and prompts is a simple and guided start into a better understanding of your Self and your Shadow.

This process might make you uncomfortable, and indirectly, this is the whole point. These prompts have been created to engage your Shadow and encourage you to explore your feelings, emotions and potential toxic traits within yourself.

No one enjoys being called out, so just remember this is a personal journey of self discovery into becoming the best and most aware version of yourself.

Be honest and be kind to yourself.
Know that you are enough and you are worth it.

A person is whole only when they take into account their shadow.

– Djuna Barnes

answering the prompts

These questions are the start of understanding who you are as a whole. They are simple and yet difficult questions to answer.

Consider only answering one prompt at a time and at your own pace. This will allow you to fully explore your consciousness. There is no timeframe or order in which you need to finish the prompts for your Shadow Work, however the Healing Work prompts are intended to be answered at the end of your Shadow Work journey.

Find a time where you can be uninterrupted and create a space of comfort; light a candle, silence your notifications, quietly play some of your favourite music, and keep the outside distractions minimal. This is your time.

When writing your answers, there has never been a better time to be raw and truthful. Being honest with yourself is harder if you think someone else is going to judge you for your honesty. Understand that this journal and the experiences you gain from it are for you and you alone.

Processing what you're learning about yourself can be daunting. Whenever we experience something difficult, a moment of self-care is always recommended afterwards to heal, reflect and to grow.

Everything that irritates us
about others can lead us to a
better understanding of ourselves.
– Carl Jung

shadow work

WHAT DOES THE PHRASE "SHADOW WORK" MEAN TO YOU? WHAT DO YOU WANT TO TAKE AWAY FROM IT?

WHAT ARE THREE THINGS YOU WANT TO ACHIEVE WITH YOUR SHADOW WORK?

WHAT ARE YOUR CORE VALUES? ARE YOU FULFILLING THEM?

WHAT IS YOUR DEFINITION OF FAILURE?
HOW DOES FAILING MAKE YOU FEEL?

WHAT IS A PERSONALITY TRAIT THAT YOU WISHED YOU POSSESSED? WHY IS THAT?

HOW DOES CONFRONTATION MAKE YOU FEEL?

WRITE ABOUT A TIME YOU FELT LET DOWN.
HOW DID THIS MAKE YOU FEEL?
WAS YOUR REACTION RATIONAL?

WHAT IS THE BIGGEST LIE YOU TELL YOURSELF? WHY?

Your shadow is here for a reason.
Not so much to terrify or invalidate you,
but to help you see what you're afraid of and
to teach you how to tame that fear.
- Helen S. Rosenau

WHEN DO YOU FEEL THE MOST CONFIDENT?
WHAT IS STOPPING YOU FROM
FEELING THAT WAY MOST OF THE TIME?

HOW DO YOU FEEL ABOUT WHO YOU ARE AS A PERSON? WHY?

WHO HAS DISAPPOINTED YOU THE MOST IN YOUR LIFE? ARE THEY STILL IN YOUR LIFE? WHY?

HOW WERE YOU TAUGHT TO DEAL WITH EMOTIONS AS A CHILD OR TEEN? HOW DO YOU PROCESS YOUR EMOTIONS NOW?

CAN YOU SAY WITH COMPLETE HONESTY THAT YOU RESPECT THE BOUNDARIES OF OTHERS?

WHAT IS THE WORST EMOTION TO EXPERIENCE FOR YOU? WHY? WHERE DOES THAT COME FROM?

WHO INFLUENCES YOU THE MOST?
ARE THEY AWARE OF THAT INFLUENCE?
DESCRIBE YOUR RELATIONSHIP
WITH THIS PERSON.

WHAT MAKES YOU FEEL VALUED?

Every pain, addiction, anguish, longing, depression, anger or fear is an orphaned part of us seeking joy, some disowned shadow wanting to return to the light and home of ourselves.

- Jacob Nordby

WHAT DO PEOPLE OFTEN MISUNDERSTAND ABOUT YOU? HOW DOES THIS MAKE YOU FEEL?

DO YOU HAVE HEALTHY BOUNDARIES IN YOUR RELATIONSHIPS? ARE THERE RELATIONSHIPS THAT HAVE STRONGER BOUNDARIES THAN OTHERS?

WHAT DOES FREEDOM MEAN TO YOU?

WHAT WAS THE LAST ARGUMENT YOU HAD?
WAS IT RESOLVED?
IF NOT, WHAT IS STOPPING YOU
FROM RESOLVING IT?

WHAT IS YOUR LOVE LANGUAGE?
HOW DO YOU WANT TO BE LOVED?

DESCRIBE YOUR RELATIONSHIP WITH YOUR PARENTS/PARENTAL FIGURES AS A CHILD. HAS IT CHANGED AS YOU GREW UP? WHY DO YOU THINK THIS IS?

WHAT BEHAVIORS ARE YOU MOST JUDGEMENTAL OF? IS THIS JUSTIFIED?

HOW DO YOU TEND TO RESPOND TO COMPLIMENTS?

It is essential, now more than ever, to bravely gaze into the darkest chambers of our hearts. It is only with an honest appraisal of the seat of our souls that we can mend ourselves individually and collectively.

– Sasha Graham

HOW DO YOU REACT WHEN YOU'RE ANGRY? DO YOU RECOGNIZE THESE TRAITS IN SOMEONE WHO WAS CLOSE TO YOU GROWING UP?

WHAT IS THE MOST HURTFUL THING YOU HAVE DONE TO YOURSELF?

WHO ARE YOU MOST GRATEFUL FOR HAVING IN YOUR LIFE? WHY?

WHAT TENDS TO TRIGGER ENVY FOR YOU? WHY DO YOU THINK THIS IS?

WHAT MAKES YOU FEEL NOT GOOD ENOUGH? WHY DO YOU THINK THIS?

WHAT TOXIC TRAITS HAVE YOU RECOGNISED IN YOUR PARENTS/PARENTAL FIGURES? HOW AND WHEN DID YOU REALIZE THIS? DO YOU POSSESS ANY OF THESE TRAITS YOURSELF?

DO YOU ALLOW YOURSELF SUFFICIENT TIME FOR SELF CARE? WHY OR WHY NOT?

WHAT MAKES YOU UNAPOLOGETICALLY HAPPY? WHY?

Your Shadow is a dark omen, a powerful teacher that reveals to you the places in your life here you are energetically blocked. When you continue to ignore these signs, you perpetuate the cycle of your suffering.

– Mateo Sol

WHAT IS YOUR INITIAL REACTION TO THE QUESTION, "DO PEOPLE RESPECT YOU"? WHY DO YOU FEEL LIKE YOU REACT THAT WAY?

DO YOU HOLD GRUDGES?
WHAT DO YOU STRUGGLE TO LET GO OF?

WHAT IS YOUR PRIORITY IN A CONNECTION WITH SOMEONE?

ARE YOU CODEPENDENT WITH ANYONE IN YOUR LIFE? WHY OR WHY NOT? HOW DOES THIS MAKE YOU FEEL?

IS THERE ANYTHING IN YOUR LIFE YOU FEEL YOU NEED TO BE FORGIVEN FOR? WHAT ARE THEY AND WHY?

HOW DO YOU FILL YOUR TIME WHEN YOU'RE BORED? ARE THEY HEALTHY HABITS?

WHAT IS THE MOST HURTFUL THING YOU HAVE EVER DONE TO SOMEONE? DO YOU JUSTIFY YOUR ACTIONS?

DO YOU HAVE RELATIONSHIPS IN YOUR LIFE THAT NO LONGER SERVE YOU? HOW DO YOU THINK YOU'D FEEL IF YOU LET THOSE RELATIONSHIPS GO? ARE THEY WORTH SAVING? WHY?

When we are aware of our weaknesses or negative tendencies, we open the opportunity to work on them.

– Allan Lokos

WHAT WAS THE LAST RELATIONSHIP OR FRIENDSHIP YOU WALKED AWAY FROM? HOW DID YOU FEEL LETTING GO? HOW DID YOU KNOW IT NEEDED TO END?

WHAT DO YOU WISH YOU COULD CHANGE ABOUT YOUR EMOTIONAL SELF? CAN YOU CHANGE IT? WHY CAN'T YOU ACCEPT THIS PART OF YOURSELF?

WHEN YOU'RE ALONE, IS YOUR INNER VOICE POSITIVE OR NEGATIVE? WHY DO YOU THINK THIS IS? IS THIS YOUR VOICE OR A VOICE INFLUENCED BY SOMEONE IN YOUR LIFE?

DOES ANYONE IN YOUR LIFE MOCK OR IGNORE YOUR EMOTIONS? HOW DO YOU RESPOND TO THIS?

WHAT ARE FIVE THINGS THAT ARE STOPPING YOU FROM BEING TRULY HAPPY? HOW CAN YOU CHANGE THIS?

WHAT DO YOU WISH YOU COULD CHANGE ABOUT YOUR PHYSICAL SELF? CAN YOU CHANGE IT? WHY CAN'T YOU ACCEPT THIS PART OF YOURSELF?

WHAT WAS THE WORST TIME YOU'VE BEEN TAKEN ADVANTAGE OF? WHY DO YOU THINK THEY DID IT?

DO YOU FEEL LESS THAN, BETTER THAN, OR EQUAL TO OTHERS? WHY?

If you don't accept yourself, you can't
transcend yourself and the world:
first, you need to increase your awareness,
then you need to accept what you learn,
then you need to take action.
- Oli Anderson

REFLECT ON YOUR FRIENDSHIPS.
WHICH ONES MAKE YOU FEEL SAFE AND LOVED?
ARE THERE ANY THAT YOU FEEL PRESSURED OR UNCOMFORTABLE WITH?

ARE YOU GOOD AT ASKING FOR HELP? DO YOU BELIEVE ASKING FOR HELP IS A STRENGTH OR WEAKNESS?

HAVE YOU EXPERIENCED CHILDHOOD TRAUMA?
HOW DO YOU THINK THAT SHAPED YOU?

WHAT KEEPS YOU FROM SPEAKING YOUR TRUTH? HOW DOES THIS MAKE YOU FEEL?

LIST OUT YOUR PARENTS/PARENTAL FIGURES' TOP FIVE VALUES, HABITS OR BELIEFS. THEN LIST YOURS. ARE THEY THE SAME? WHY OR WHY NOT?

WHAT IS YOUR TRIGGER FOR EXPERIENCING FEAR? WHY?

WHAT PARTS OF YOUR LIFE ARE YOU UNHAPPY WITH? WHAT DO YOU FEEL YOU NEED TO DO IN ORDER TO CHANGE THIS?

DO YOU HAVE ANY TRAITS THAT ARE TAKEN FOR GRANTED? HOW DOES THIS MAKE YOU FEEL?

Shadow Work enables us to alter our self-sabotaging behavior so that we can achieve a more self-directed life.

- Connie Zweig

WHAT ARE THE TELLTALE SIGNS THAT YOUR MENTAL HEALTH IS WEAKENING?

DO YOU FIND YOURSELF OVER-THINKING SOMETHING YOU'VE DONE OR SAID? WHAT TRIGGERS THIS?

WHAT MEMORY BRINGS YOU SHAME? WHAT LED TO THIS BEHAVIOR?

HOW CAN YOU LEARN TO BE THANKFUL FOR WHAT HAS HAPPENED TO YOU IN YOUR LIFE?

ARE YOU CURRENTLY ADDICTED TO ANYTHING THAT YOU THINK YOU COULD BENEFIT FROM HAVING LESS OF IN YOUR LIFE? WHAT IS STOPPING YOU?

IN THE LAST YEAR HAVE YOU CHANGED AT ALL FOR THE BETTER?

WHO ARE YOU MOST JEALOUS OF?

WHICH PERSONALITY TRAITS DO YOU THINK WOULD BE THE WORST TO HAVE? WHY DO YOU FEEL THIS WAY?

Our wounds are often the openings into the best and most beautiful part of us.

– David Richo

DO YOU EVER EXPERIENCE A PHYSICAL REACTION TO NEGATIVE EMOTIONS? WHAT ARE THEY AND WHY DO YOU THINK THAT IS?

WHAT HAS BEEN YOUR BIGGEST REGRET IN LIFE? WILL YOU EVER BE ABLE TO MAKE PEACE WITH YOUR CHOICE?

DO YOU LOOK UP TO OR ADMIRE ANYONE? WHO IS THAT AND WHY?

WHY DO YOU HESITATE TO BE KIND TO YOURSELF? WHERE DO YOU THINK THIS HESITATION COMES FROM?

REFLECT ON THE UNHEALTHY RELATIONSHIPS YOU HAVE CURRENTLY OR HAVE HAD. IS THERE A THEME? WHY DO YOU THINK YOU FIND YOURSELF IN THESE? HOW CAN YOU AVOID THEM?

DO YOU MAKE FUN OF YOURSELF
TO ENTERTAIN OTHERS?
WHY DO YOU THINK THIS IS?

THINK ABOUT A TIME SOMEONE BROKE YOUR TRUST. WHAT HAPPENED? WHAT WOULD YOU SAY TO THIS PERSON?

WHAT HABITS DO YOU FEEL YOU NEED TO STOP? WHY?

You don't find light by
avoiding the darkness.
- S. Kelley Harrell

WHAT GIVES YOU A SENSE OF PURPOSE?
IS THIS LACKING IN YOUR LIFE?
HOW CAN YOU MAKE MORE OF IT?

DO YOU JUDGE MORE EASILY THAN YOU ACCEPT? WHY DO YOU THINK THIS IS?

WHAT IS THE HARDEST LESSON YOU'VE HAD TO LEARN THIS LAST YEAR?

WHAT DO YOU LOVE THE MOST ABOUT YOUR LIFE?

DO YOU FIND YOURSELF ADAPTING YOUR PERSONA TO FIT IN WITH A PERSON/SITUATION? WHAT WOULD HAPPEN IF YOU SHARED YOUR TRUE SELF? HOW DOES THIS MAKE YOU FEEL?

WHEN WAS THE LAST TIME YOU EXPERIENCED SELF-DESTRUCTIVE BEHAVIOUR? WHAT CAUSED THIS?

ARE YOU CURRENTLY ANGRY ABOUT SOMETHING? WHAT HAPPENED?

DO YOU HAVE ANY UNREALISTIC EXPECTATIONS OF YOURSELF? WHO EMBEDDED THESE EXPECTATIONS IN YOU?

Our work is to integrate and eventually transcend darkness and light altogether by holding them equally in a state of interconnection.

– Sasha Graham

WHEN WAS THE LAST TIME YOU FAILED AT SOMETHING? HOW DID YOU REACT? COULD YOUR REACTION BE BETTER?

DO YOU HAVE A RELIGION OR SPIRITUALITY? WHAT IS YOUR RELATIONSHIP WITH IT?

DESCRIBE A SITUATION WHERE YOU HAVE BEEN A HYPOCRITE. WHY DID YOU ALLOW THIS? WHAT WOULD YOU CHANGE IF YOU COULD GO BACK?

WHAT DOES HAPPINESS MEAN TO YOU?

ARE YOU CURRENTLY HOLDING ONTO ANY MEMORIES OR TRAUMAS THAT ARE PREVENTING YOU FROM MOVING FORWARD? WHAT IS TRULY STOPPING YOU FROM LETTING THEM GO?

DO YOU WORRY ABOUT YOUR FUTURE? WHY?

HOW IS YOUR RELATIONSHIP WITH YOUR MOTHER/MOTHER FIGURE?

HOW IS YOUR RELATIONSHIP WITH YOUR FATHER/FATHER FIGURE?

The person you call an enemy is an
exaggerated aspect of your own shadow self.
- Deepak Chopra

IF YOU HAVE SIBLINGS, HOW IS THEIR RELATIONSHIP WITH YOUR PARENTS/PARENTAL FIGURES DIFFERENT FROM YOURS? WHY IS THIS?

HOW OFTEN DO YOU EXPERIENCE SADNESS? WHY IS THIS?

WHAT PARTS OF YOUR LIFE DO YOU FEEL YOU NEED TO ADDRESS FIRST? WHY?
WHAT DO YOU THINK WILL HAPPEN WHEN YOU COMPLETE THEM?

ARE THERE ANY PATTERNS IN YOUR LIFE THAT YOU FIND YOURSELF REPEATING?

WRITE THE WORDS OR MESSAGE THAT YOU NEED TO HEAR TODAY.

WHAT WAYS DO YOU SHOW UP FOR OTHERS BUT FAIL TO FOR YOURSELF? WHY IS THIS?

WHEN DID YOU LAST RUN AWAY FROM YOUR RESPONSIBILITIES? WHAT HAPPENED?

ARE YOU PRETENDING TO BE ANYONE? WHY?

This thing of darkness I acknowledge mine.
- William Shakespeare

DO YOU RELATE TO A FICTIONAL CHARACTER? WHO IS IT AND WHY? WHAT PARTS OF THEM DO YOU SEE IN YOURSELF?

WHO IS A PART OF YOUR INNER CIRCLE? IS THERE A THEME THAT THEY SHARE?

DO YOU TRULY HONOUR YOUR FEELINGS?

ARE YOU WHERE YOU THOUGHT YOU'D BE AT THIS POINT IN YOUR LIFE? IF YES, WHAT IS YOUR NEXT GOAL? IF NOT, CAN YOU ACCEPT WHERE YOU CURRENTLY ARE? WHY OR WHY NOT?

Grow your magic from your struggle.

- E.R. King

healing work

HOW DO YOU FEEL HAVING FINISHED THE JOURNAL?

HOW DID YOU DEMONSTRATE SELF-CARE AFTER PARTS OF THE JOURNAL WERE DIFFICULT TO ANSWER?

WHAT PARTS OF YOURSELF DO YOU WANT TO WORK ON FIRST?

WHAT WAS THE HARDEST QUESTION TO ANSWER? WHY?

DO YOU FORGIVE YOURSELF?

HOW DO YOU PLAN TO MOVE FORWARD IF YOU EXPERIENCE ONE OF YOUR SHADOW TRAITS?

IF BY CHANCE ANYONE WERE TO COME ACROSS THIS JOURNAL, WHAT IS THE ONE THING YOU WOULD WANT THEM TO KNOW ABOUT YOU AND YOUR SHADOW WORK EXPERIENCE?

WRITE YOUR PAST SELF A LETTER, DEMONSTRATING APOLOGY, UNDERSTANDING AND FORGIVENESS.

WRITE YOUR CURRENT SELF A LOVE LETTER.

Our wounds are often the openings into the best and most beautiful part of us.

– David Richo

NOTES

NOTES

NOTES

NOTES

www.ingramcontent.com/pod-product-compliance
Lightning Source LLC
Chambersburg PA
CBHW061219210726
48294CB00006B/1902

* 9 7 8 1 7 7 7 4 9 1 8 2 6 *